THE TEN COMMANDMENTS

THE TEN COMMANDMENTS

TAN Books
Charlotte, North Carolina

Scripture quotations are from the Catholic Edition of the Revised Standard Version of the Bible, copyright © 1965, 1966 National Council of Churches of Christ in the United States of America. Used by permission. All rights reserved.

Cover design by Caroline Kiser.

ISBN: 978-1-61890-629-8

Published in the United States by
TAN Books
PO Box 410487
Charlotte, NC 28241
www.TANBooks.com

Printed and bound in the United States of America

CONTENTS

CONTENTS

INTRODUCTION

Think not that I have come to abolish the law and the prophets; I have come not to abolish them but to fulfill them . . . unless your righteousness exceeds that of the scribes and Pharisees, you will never enter the kingdom of heaven (Mt 5:17, 20) These words of Jesus remind us of the interpretive key to the Law which we discussed in the last flier. The scribes and the Pharisees of Jesus' time interpreted the Law in strictly legal fashion. This led them to understand each commandment is a minimalist fashion. The command not to kill was understood as only a law against the unjust taking of life. It meant purely and simply that we were not to murder. But Jesus says we must move beyond such a narrow view and He interprets the Law more fully from the standpoint of love: *You have heard that it was said to the men of old, 'You shall not kill . . . But I say to you that every one who is angry with his brother shall be liable to judgment; whoever insults his brother shall be liable to the council, and whoever says, 'You fool!' shall be liable to the hell of fire.* (Mt 5:21–22). Thus, for Jesus the Commandment, "You shall not kill" is about more than just taking life. It is about all the attitudes and evil deeds that lead to murder: wrathful anger, attitudes of contempt, revenge, bitterness, and hatred. Jesus asks us to consider all the implications of God's Law. He does this because we are called into a relationship of love and trust of God. God commands us and sets limits for us not because He is out to make life difficult or to take away our fun. God commands because he loves us and does not want us to be trapped in the painful realities of sin and evil. Through the grace He gives us Jesus enables us to trust the Father and to love Him. Love does not treat the law as an imposition but as a gift. Love does not seek to avoid the Law by asking, "What is the least I can do to just get by?" Love's response is extravagant. It embraces the Law and asks, "What more can I do?" This is the disposition of heart that Jesus gives us by his grace. As we examine each commandment we will apply Jesus' interpretive principal.

We will look at the fuller and inner meaning of each command and see the freedom and truth to which each command points. We do this in trust of God who does not command without first giving us the grace, the power, to keep what He mandates (*cf.* 1 Cor 10:13). As a final preliminary comment, note how Jesus points to love as the foundation of the commandments. *And one of them, a lawyer, asked him a question, to test him. "Teacher, which is the great commandment in the law?" And he said to him, "You shall love the Lord your God with all your heart, and with all your soul, and with all your mind. This is the great and first commandment. And a second is like it, You shall love your neighbor as yourself. On these two commandments depend all the law and the prophets* (Mt 22:37ff). Love contains the whole law. A man who loves his wife does not need a command that says, "Do not break her arm." One who loves already understands this. The twofold summary of the Law by Jesus on the basis of love also helps us to sort out the Ten Commandments. The first three commandments specify the command to love God absolutely. The remaining seven spell out what it means to love our neighbor. We are now ready to look at the first commandment.

THE FIRST COMMANDMENT

I AM THE LORD YOUR GOD.
YOU SHALL NOT HAVE
STRANGE GODS BEFORE ME.

I am the Lord your God: you shall not have strange gods before me (Ex 20:2–17; Dt 5:6–2). Is God merely jealous here? Why is he so exclusive in his demand to be worshiped? Perhaps the best way to understand this commandment is to understand that God seeks to protect us from false claimants to our worship and obedience. The history of the ancient world shows a long sad history of the confusion that arises from the false gods, which had influence. Some of these false religions and cults demanded human sacrifice, many enshrined bizarre sexual practices and called for

1

numerous and costly sacrifices. Most of them also fostered fears and superstitions to hold their power over people. The Greeks even had an altar to the "unknown god" (*cf.* Acts 17:23) and offered worship just in case such a god existed and he (or she), angry at not being worshiped, would seek to bring about destruction of some kind. There were many confusing and contradictory claims and demands that bewildered much of the ancient world. Even if these ancient religions contained some elements of the truth, they were incomplete expressions of the truth and contained numerous errors. Though too lengthy to reproduce here, a rather vivid and terrifying description of the evils and sorrows resulting from false worship is given in Rom 1:18*ff.*

In the first commandment, God seeks to preserve His people from such bewilderment and sorrow. He alone is the Creator Lord who made all things. We can and must trust Him in all things for he is able. He gives us the one and only truth by which we may be saved. Since He alone is all-powerful we need not worry of the anger or power of other gods for if they exist at all, *the Lord our God is God of gods and Lord of lords* (Dt 10:17). God therefore speaks to us in love and commands us to worship Him alone, to trust him in all things and serve him by our obedience. *Only in God will my soul be at rest; from him comes my salvation. He only is my rock and my salvation, my fortress; I shall not be greatly moved.* (Ps 62:1–2).

Implications of the 1ˢᵗ Commandment

The first commandment is much more than a law against worshiping idols. It is a summons to a whole way of life. God calls us to the absolute obedience of faith in Him who is faithful just, and trustworthy without any evil. We ought therefore to accept his words and have complete faith in him and not fail to acknowledge God is merciful, infinitely good, and all-powerful. So we should place our hope in him and be grateful for the goodness and love he has poured out on us. In the Scriptures this is often recalled when at the beginning or end of reciting some aspect of the Law, the phrase 'I am the Lord.' Is used. It is God's way of saying, 'It is I, the Lord who loves you and provides for you who speak this to you. Trust me' (see *CCC* 2086)

Since faith is such an important response to the first commandment it also follows that we must nourish and protect our faith with prudence and vigilance, and to reject everything that is opposed to it. Many today take lightly the duty to know the sacred truths of our faith revealed by God. Yet many of these same individuals have detailed and through knowledge of worldly matters. Though it is not wrong to learn of the things of this world, when it is paired with a willful neglecting of the truths revealed by God may well show where our true priorities lie and exhibit a form of idolatry. Idolatry refers to false pagan worship and consists in considering divine what is not God. We do this when revere a creature in place of God, This could by revering what others consider as gods or by worshipping demons (as Satanists do), but it can also including treating power, pleasure, money or popularity as idols. (see *CCC* 2112).

The duty to adore and worship

Another important duty flowing from the first commandment is the call to love and worship God. We ought to adore God, we ought to acknowledge him as our Creator and Savior, He is the Lord and Maker of everything that exists, and every good thing manifests his infinite and merciful Love. So Scripture says, "You shall worship the Lord your God, and him only shall you serve," (see *CCC* 2095; Dt 6:13; Lk 4:8). Thus every human being has a solemn obligation to worship God through prayer and praise, both public and private. Our prayer and praise must come from true dispositions of the heart.

However we are also warned against superstition which attributes the effectiveness of prayers, sacraments or sacramentals to their mere external performance, without reference the interior dispositions that are necessary. (see *CCC* 2111)

Attempted Control

A common sin against the first commandment is the attempt to tell the future or to control it. While God can reveal the future to prophets or saints. This is rare and still demands faith of us. A better Christian attitude is to grow in confident trust of God's providence, rather than cultivating an unhealthy curiosity about the future. (*CCC* 2115).

Further to be excluded are the *consulting of horoscopes, palm reading, clairvoyance, and recourse to mediums. The sinful drive underlying these sins is a desire for power over time and history, and other human beings, as well as a fascination with hidden powers. Only God should receive our honor, respect, and loving fear.* (see *CCC* 2116).

Atheism

Many individuals today either do not perceive or explicitly reject the existence of God or consider His bond to us to be unimportant. The catechism calls this one of the most serious problems of our time. Atheism comes in different forms. One is the practical materialism which insists that the only valid needs, aspirations, and sciences are material concerns of the here and now. Atheistic humanism thinks of man as an end in himself, or even the sole maker and determiner of right and wrong, with supreme authority and autonomy. Yet another form of contemporary atheism thinks in utopian terms that the liberation of man can be possible merely by economic and social liberation. (see *CCC* 2124) All forms of Atheism entertain a false and exaggerated conception of human autonomy, refusing dependence on God. (see *CCC* 2126).

Agnosticism is a related matter except that the agnostic, instead of denying God's existence outright, declares that it is impossible to know if God exists or not. This of course is a denial of revelation in the Bible and in creation.

Believers can have a lot to do with the rise of atheism. If we are careless about our instruction in the faith, or present its teaching falsely, or fail in our religious, moral, or social life, we often conceal and distort the faith rather than reveal the true nature of God and faith (see *CCC* 2125).

In the end the first commandment brings before us the truth about God. He alone is God and Lord. To him alone belong all worship, honor, praise, and thanksgiving. Since he is all-powerful and loving we can trust Him and begin to live as children who are both blessed and loved. It is by this First Commandment that we cling to our God and entrust our whole self to Him. In the depths of our hearts a song sounds forth that is a fruit of this first and greatest commandment: God is a good God. He is a great God. He can do anything but fail. He can move so many mountains our of our way. God is a wonderful God.

THE SECOND COMMANDMENT

YOU SHALL NOT TAKE THE NAME
OF THE LORD YOUR GOD IN VAIN.

At first glance this commandment is easy enough to understand. We must have respect for the Lord's name. But we might wonder as to why a name is so important that God would devote one of the Ten Commandments to it. To understand this we must recall that in the ancient world and among the Jewish people the disclosure of a name belonged to the order of trust and intimacy. Though individuals could be publicly known by their surname, title or occupation, personal names were shared only among close friends or family. We retain some of this custom in the way that we usually expect children to address adults not by their first names but by their title or by their title and last name. Thus it was a great gift and honor that the eternal, awesome and unchanging God should reveal his name to us. Our response to this must always be one of gratitude and of silent loving adoration of his name. We should not introduce it into speech except to bless, praise and glorify.

Cursing & Blasphemy

It is clear that to use the name of God the Father or the Lord Jesus to curse, condemn or berate others is wholly inappropriate. Many people call this "swearing" though to be precise, "swearing" involves taking an oath. We might better call this cursing or blasphemy.

Blasphemy consists in uttering against God words of hatred, reproach or defiance. This may be done inwardly or outwardly. Also related to the sin of blasphemy is speaking ill of God or of failing to respect him in our speech.

Blasphemy and vain use of God's name are hardly rare today. When we consider the movies, books, and music of our own day it is shocking to consider how frequently the Name of the Lord is used profanely. Directors and authors often claim they must include such language to reflect an accurate portrait of real human interactions. Sadly there is some truth in their claim. We clearly live in a society that is increasingly contemptuous of God's great and glorious name. This is why each of us should consider how we might be more faithful to the second commandment.

The wider meaning of "vain"

This is why it is also important to reflect on the meaning of the word "vain" Vain means "empty" or "insincere." Thus we should avoid using God's name in an empty fashion. The most common way this is done is by expressions such as "Oh my God!" or "Lord!" Such an expressions are usually not meant to be irreverent. But they are most often said in an unreflective manner that reduces God's name to a mere expression of surprise or exasperation. In some, the habit of using this expression is so ingrained that they are hardly aware that they are doing it. This makes it a "vain" or empty use of the name of God and it is clearly not the ideal to which the second commandment draws us. The name of God is to be used with great reverence and in a reflective, prayerful manner, *O Lord how excellent is thy name in all the earth!*

The swearing of oaths

A final but very important area of consideration in terms of the second commandment is the swearing of oaths. Swearing an oath in God's name is to take God as a witness to what one affirms. It also calls upon divine truthfulness as a pledge of one's own truthfulness. When it is truthful and legitimate an oath highlights the relationship of human speech with God's truth. A false oath however calls God to be witness to a lie and is absolutely contrary to the holiness of the divine name. Jesus urges great caution in making oaths (Mt 5:33–34) but following St. Paul (2 Cor 1:23; Gal 1:20), the tradition of the Church has understood Jesus words as not excluding oaths made for grave and right reasons (for example in court).

In all our words and actions we are called to honor the name of the Lord. Knowing God's name is a sign that God has deigned to enter into an intimate, personal relationship with us. This should inspire gratitude, reverence, and love. Each time the divine name sounds in our ears or stirs within our souls there should sweep over us an immense feeling of love and of being loved. *Blessed be the name of the Lord!*

THE THIRD COMMANDMENT

REMEMBER THAT YOU KEEP HOLY
THE SABBATH DAY.

Remember the Sabbath day to keep it holy. Six days shall labor, and do all your work; but the seventh day is a Sabbath to the Lord your God; in it you shall not do any work.

Of all the commandments, it might seem we would get this one right. After all it commands us to rest one day, the Sabbath, each week. Yet many today find this a difficult commandment to observe. More and more, Sunday (which according to Apostolic Tradition is the day on which Christians fulfill this commandment) is more often a day of shopping and numerous activities. This also makes it a day of work for many who staff stores, restaurants, theaters, and the like. What is the purpose of this commandment and why was it so important that God devoted a commandment to it?

God's own example

The first reason for this commandment under-scores the fact that we are made in the image and likeness of God. Thus we are to rest on the seventh day because God did so in his work of creation: *Six days you shall labor, and do all your work; but the seventh day is a Sabbath to the LORD your God; in it you shall not do any work, you, or your son, or your daughter, your manservant, or your maidservant, or your cattle, or the sojourner who is within your gates; for in six days the LORD made heaven and earth, the sea, and all that is in them, and rested the seventh day; therefore the LORD blessed the Sabbath day and hallowed it.* (Ex 20:9–11). Thus God's rest is the model for our rest. Since God rested on the seventh day so should we. In so resting we ought to let others rest and be refreshed, especially the poor. The Sabbath brings the grind of every day work to a halt and brings the pause that refreshes. Scripture even speaks of the Sabbath as a day of protest against the servitude o\f work and the wor-ship of money (e.g. Neh 13:15–22; Amos 8:4–6).

A day of rest

All of this is an important reminder to us. We tend to judge our value based on what we do and what we have. But God has written the need for rest deeply in our being. If we live healthy lives we will sleep one third of our day (8 hours). Even beyond this we need extended periods of rest and relaxation. And God commands us to cease striving one whole day of the week. In all these ways God bids us to see our value based on who we are and whose we are.

A day for worship

Scripture also reveals the Sabbath day as a day to recall the many and marvelous saving works of the Lord, in particular the liberation from bondage in Egypt: *You shall remember that you were a servant in the land of Egypt, and the LORD your God brought you out thence with a mighty hand and an outstretched arm; therefore the LORD your God commanded you to keep the Sabbath day.* (Dt 5:15). In this way we also begin to see the link of the Sabbath to worship. By taking time to cease our labors we are freed to consider and experience the goodness of our God and of his saving love. Thus the Sabbath is not only about rest. It is also intended for worship of God and the receiving of his blessings.

Many claim that although scripture mandates a day of rest, there is no requirement to attend Church. But this is really not the case. Scripture links the Sabbath to "sacred assembly." For example, *Six days shall work be done; but the seventh day is a Sabbath of solemn rest and sacred assembly; you shall do no work; it is a Sabbath to the LORD.* (Lv 23:3). Thus, notice how this text spells out that the Sabbath is not only for rest but for "sacred assembly." This phrase, "sacred assembly" is what is meant by the word "Church." Church means "assembly."

Likewise, Jesus in his observance of Sabbath attended the synagogue (another word for "assembly" or "gathering"). Scripture says Jesus attended the synagogue on the Sabbath habitually (*cf.* Lk 4:16).

Further, scripture admonishes us, to *not neglect to meet together, as is the habit of some, but encourage one another* (Heb 10:25).

For some to say that they don't need to assemble, to meet together with fellow Christians in Church on Sunday, (our Sabbath) is surely unbiblical. The Old Testament commanded it, Jesus attended, who are we to fail in this regard?

We must not neglect to meet together. We must not neglect to receive Holy Communion and be instructed in the Word of God.

For these reasons, in accordance with scriptures and sound reasoning, the Church obliges all the Catholic faithful in good health to attend Mass every Sunday.

A further indication that Sunday Church worship is required of the Christian is in Jesus mandate that we receive Holy Communion. Jesus warns us not to miss receiving the Holy Communion with these words: *Unless you eat the flesh of the Son of Man and drink his blood you have no life in you.* (Jn 6:53) Without the Holy Eucharist which is the Body and Blood of Jesus, we are starving ourselves spiritually. If you and I were to stop eating our worldly food we would soon grow weak and eventually die. It would be a form of suicide. It is no less true of our spiritual food. If we stop receiving the Body and Blood of Jesus in Holy Communion, we grow weak and eventually die, spiritually, we "have no life in us!" To skip Sunday Mass sets up a deadly pattern of spiritual starvation, it is a deadly thing, a mortal sin! For this reason the Church teaches: *the faithful are obliged to participate in the Eucharist on days of obligation, unless excused for a serious reason (for example, illness,*

the care of infants) or dispensed by their own pastor.
Those who deliberately fail in this obligation com-
mit a grave sin. (CCC 2181) It comes down to this,
either we eat or we die.

Perhaps Jesus had this in mind when he told a
Parable about a King who gave a banquet for his
Son: *The kingdom of heaven may be compared to*
a king who gave a marriage feast for his son, ³and
sent his servants to call those who were invited to
the marriage feast; but they would not come. ⁴Again
he sent other servants, saying, "Tell those who are
invited, Behold, I have made ready my dinner, my
oxen and my fat calves are killed, and everything is
ready; come to the marriage feast." ⁵But they made
light of it and went off, one to his farm, another
to his business, ⁶while the rest seized his servants,
treated them shamefully, and killed them. ⁷The king
was angry, and he sent his troops and destroyed
those murderers and burned their city. (Mt 22:2ff)

God's admonitions concerning the Sabbath
make sense. Far too many suffer stressful, hec-
tic lives driven by chaotic demands with little
or no relief in sight. God, like a good physician
orders rest and thanksgiving. Jesus reminds us
that the Sabbath was made *for* man (Mk 2:27).
Thus, while he dismissed the excessively legalistic
interpretations of the meaning of rest in his day,

he always upheld the importance and necessity of the Sabbath and observed it himself.

A call to trust.

In the end, the call to keep the Sabbath holy is a call to trust. Although it might seem that rest is a natural human tendency, it will also be seen that the opposite is more often true. Many fears accompany the cessation of work: Will competitors surpass me while I rest? Will I fail to complete all my duties? Will others amass more wealth or power while I fall behind? How can I pay all my bills or finance my lifestyle if I do not work more hours? Will my children's college education be possible if I do not work every day? Will I loose my job or not get one at all if I do not agree to work Sundays?

In effect God says, "I want you to trust me. Take one day and set it aside entirely. Do no work on that day. Cease striving, let go of the controls. Rest, worship, consider your blessings, enjoy them and give thanks for them. Spend time with your family and friends. I promise you that you will accomplish more with the six days remaining that you ever would with all seven. Understand and trust that if you are faithful to my commandment to rest and worship on the Sabbath

I will bless you." (*cf.* Jer 17:24; Is 56:4; Dt 28:9ff; Ex 19:5). The gift of our time to God is a precious one indeed. But why should we fear to give it to the author of all time? Trust in God.

And remember, says the Lord: *Unless you eat my flesh and drink my blood, you have no life in you.* (Jn 6:53)

THE FOURTH COMMANDMENT

HONOR YOUR FATHER
AND
YOUR MOTHER.

The fourth commandment opens what is called the "second table of the Ten Commandments." The first table of the Law consists in how we must honor, love, and obey God. The remaining seven commandments all deal with the love and respect due to our neighbor. Since Charity begins at home, the fourth commandment places essential emphasis on family love. God has willed that, after him, we should honor our parents to whom we owe our life and who have handed on to us the knowledge of God.

The wide scope of this Commandment

While it is true that charity begins at home it is also true that it does not end there. So also the fourth commandment is about more than honoring our parents. The wording of the fourth command-ment focuses on children in their relationship to their father and mother. But is also addresses relationships in the extended family and requires honor, and gratitude for elders, teachers, employ-ers, and leaders. It also directs citizens to a proper love of their country, and respect and coopera-tion toward those who administer or govern it. (see *CCC* 2199) In examining this Commandment it will be beneficial for us to look first at the family and then to enlarge our scope to the wider societal implications.

An important clarification.

Before examining the duties of children there is an important premise underlying this command-ment and which must not be overlooked: parents and all those in authority have obligations and duties that flow from their status. To overlook or ignore these obligations places significant burdens upon children, subordinates, and others. This in turn can lead to bewilderment and contributes to an undermining of the respect and honor which ought ordinarily be paid parents, elders, and those in authority. Thus, while parents and lawful authorities ought to be respected it is also true to say that they must conduct themselves in a manner that is respectable and observe their duties with care. What are some of these duties? The Catechism of the Catholic Church gives a fine summary of them and the text is largely reproduced here.

The duties of parents.

While children should reverence their parents, it is also true that Parents should strive to be respectable and always remember that their children are first the children of God. In being obedient to the will of the Father in heaven, parents teach by deed as well as word. They do this first by creating a home where tenderness, forgiveness, respect, and fidelity, are lived. Parents ought to manifest sound judgment, and self-mastery. These sorts of virtues not only teach children, but also help parents to properly guide and correct children. Parents also need to protect their children from the compromising and degrading influences in culture and are the primary teachers and evangelizers of their children. They should bring them from their earliest years to the Church and explain to them the beauty of the liturgy and prayer and read them Scripture. As far as possible parents have the duty of choosing schools that will best help them in their task as Christian educators. (see *CCC* 2221–2231).

It is in the context of the fulfillment of these duties that honor and respect for parents finds it fullest meaning. Honor for one's parents ought not be experienced as a burden but as a joy and the fruit of thankfulness and mutual affection.

The duties of Children

What then are the duties of children? Here too the Catechism provides a rich summary of the meaning and implications of this commandment.

Respect for parents ought to come from a sprit of deep gratitude toward those who, have brought their children into the world and enabled them to grow in stature, wisdom, and grace. "With all your heart honor your father, and do not forget the birth pangs of your mother. Remember that through your parents you were born; what can you give back to them that equals their gift to you?" *(Sirach 7:27–28)*

Obedience

Respect is shown by and openness to being taught and obedience. "My son, keep your father's commandment, and forsake not your mother's teaching" (Prv 6:20) . . . As long as a child lives at home with his parents, he or she should obey his parents in what they. "Children, obey your parents in everything, for this pleases the Lord." (Col 3:20) Children should also obey the reasonable directions of their teachers and all to whom their parents have entrusted them. If for some good reason a child is convinced that what he or she is being told to do is morally wrong, then obedience does not apply since God is to be obeyed above all. Even as they grow up, children should continue to respect their parents, consider their needs, seek their advice, and accept their just admonitions. While obedience toward parents ends when children leave home, respect does not end. Respect is always owed to parents.

Honor and care in old age

The fourth commandment also calls for grown children to remember their responsibilities toward their parents in terms of material and moral support in old age or times of illness, and loneliness.

"Whoever honors his father atones for sins, and whoever glorifies his mother is like one who lays up treasure. Whoever honors his father will be gladdened by his own children, and when he prays he will be heard. Whoever glorifies his father will have long life, and whoever obeys the Lord will refresh his mother." (Sir 3:2–6).

Wider family implications

The fourth commandment speaks to the importance of maintaining harmony in all of family life among brothers and sisters. Proper gratitude and reverence is also due to those from whom they have received the gift of faith in the Church such as parents, godparents, other family members, pastors, catechists, teachers, and friends. (see *CCC* 2214–2220).

At the heart of civilization

It cannot be underestimated how important the family is for the very existence of society and civilization. The widespread breakdown of the family in our own time already shows the grave results that flow from such a breakdown. Can our civilization be thought secure if such a breakdown is allowed to continue?

Since the family is so important for the well-being of society, there is a particular responsibility for society to support and strengthen traditional marriage and family. Values learned in the family such as respect for authority, making stable commitments, and forming interdependent relationships form a foundation in wider culture for responsible freedom, security, and shared responsibility within society. The family is like a school in which, children can learn moral values and the proper use of freedom.

Civil authority has a grave duty protect and foster a proper notion of marriage and family, to safeguard public morality, and promote the common good. (see *CCC* 2207, 2210)

Honor all lawful authority

The fourth commandment *also requires us to honor all who have received authority in society from God.* (see *CCC* 2234)

Those who exercise authority at any level must remember they do so as God's servants and in service of God's people God. They must never command what is contrary to God's law or to the dignity of persons. They must facilitate the exercise of freedom and responsibility by all.

Authorities must command equitably, avoid favoritism, dispense justice humanely, and seek the common good as well as preserve individual rights. In all cases they must remember that they have authority only to serve (*cf.* Mt 10:37)

Citizens and those subject to authority have a duty to respect and obey lawful authority. They should see lawful authorities as, in a sense, representatives of God from whom all authority ultimately comes. They have a duty to cooperate with authorities for the building up of the common good, the securing of justice, the practice of well ordered charity, and the paying of just and reasonable taxes. The loyal collaboration to which citizens are called does not exclude the duty to voice their just criticisms and helpful advice. We are also exhorted by scripture to *offer prayers and thanksgiving for kings and all who exercise authority that we may lead a quiet and peaceable life, godly and respectable in every way* (1 Tim 2:2).

Finally, each citizen, each person under lawful authority, is obliged to follow and obey just and lawful directions and laws. However, they must not follow directives that are contrary to God's law, moral order, or fundamental human rights. Refusing obedience to civil authorities, when what they demand is contrary to an upright conscience is justified, since God is to be obeyed before any political community or leader. "Render therefore to Caesar the things that are Caesar's, and to God the things that are God's." (Mt 22:21) "We must obey God rather than men": (Acts 5:29) (see *CCC* 2242)

Here then is a good place to conclude. God is the author and origin of all authority, whether it is the authority of a parent, the authority of a work supervisor, or the authority of a governor. In honoring lawful authority we honor God who gave the authority. Jesus saw fit to remind Pontius Pilate, *You would have no power over me unless it had been given you from above* (Jn 19:11). This is a good reminder to those under authority that God stands behind duly constituted authority. But it also serves as a solemn reminder to all those in positions of authority, ultimately they are accountable to the God who is the author of their authority.

THE FIFTH COMMANDMENT

YOU SHALL NOT KILL.

The fourth Chapter of the Book of Genesis recounts the tragic story of the murder of Abel by his brother Cain. The story is an astonishing account of how evil spreads with amazing speed. The revolt of Man against God in paradise is now followed by the deadly combat of man against man. Cain was hateful and envious of his brother because God seemed more pleased with Abel's sacrifice than his own. God tries to reassure Cain but also warns him not to yield to hateful thoughts: *Sin is couching at the door; its desire is for you, but you must master it.* (Gn 4:7). Yet Cain yields to sin and to the evil one just as his parents, Adam and Eve had yielded. Cain murdered his own brother. At the root of every act of violence there is a concession to the thinking of the evil one who *was a murderer from the beginning* (Jn 8:44). God says to Cain, *What have you done? The voice of your brother's blood cries to me from the ground* (Gn 4:10). God calls Cain to reflect on the enormity of what he has done. God also reveals the regard he has for the lives of the innocent. The crime of Cain, or of any murderer, cannot go unpunished. Cain must be exiled from his land forever.

Yet even here, God underscores the sacredness of Cain's life. Cain worries that his own life will be taken in vengeance. But God declares, *If any one slays Cain, vengeance shall be taken on him sevenfold." And the Lord put a mark on Cain, lest any who came upon him should kill him* (Gn 4:15). Thus, not even a murderer loses his personal dignity. Though suitable punishment surely results, God upholds the dignity of Cain's life and calls for an end to the cycle of violence.

Human life is Sacred

The fifth commandment is not merely the forbidding of murder it is also an affirmation of the sacred character of every human life and of God's sole sovereignty over human life. Therefore as we examine the Fifth Commandment we should appreciate not only what is forbidden but also what is affirmed: the greatness and goodness of the gift of human life.

The Scriptures spell out the first and most obvious implication of the fifth commandment: *Do not slay the innocent and righteous* (Ex 23:7). It is perhaps an understatement to say that the deliberate murder of an innocent person is gravely contrary to their dignity and to God's Law. The forbidding such murder is universally valid. It obliges everyone, always and everywhere.

And yet this clear wording prompts some questions. Although murder of the innocent is always wrong, are there never cases where killing is just or necessary? What about self-defense? Police are sometimes required to use lethal force against criminals threatening public safety, is this wrong? Can criminals be executed? Isn't it sometimes necessary for nations to go to war for just and reasonable causes?

Legitimate Self-defense?

There is clearly such a thing as legitimate defense. In fact *the legitimate defense of persons and societies is not an exception to the prohibition against the murder of the innocent that constitutes intentional killing.* This is because *love toward oneself remains a fundamental principle of morality. Therefore it is legitimate to insist on respect for one's own right to life. Someone who defends his life is not guilty of murder even if he is forced to deal his aggressor a lethal blow* (CCC 2263–2264) Therefore, legitimate self-defense should not be seen as an exception to the fifth commandment but as a fulfillment of it. So, legitimate self-defense is not only a right but can be grave duty for someone, especially if they are responsible for an other's life, of the common good of the family or of the state (see CCC 2265). Thus parents, and significant leaders either of governments or other groups often have special obligations to preserve their lives. Clearly the use of lethal force to repel an attacker should be a last recourse. If non-lethal means of self-defense are available than one is obliged to use them first.

What is true for individuals is also true for the preservation of society. Criminals and aggressors must be rendered incapable of doing harm. There is a well-founded right and duty of legitimate authority to punish criminals with penalties that fit the crime. This includes, in cases of extreme gravity, the death penalty. (see CCC 2266).

The Death Penalty

Regarding the death penalty we enter into a topic about which we must be very careful. Note that the Church teaches that the death penalty may be used only in cases of "extreme gravity." The catechism was recently amended to clarify the limits of recourse to the death penalty: *If however, non-lethal means are sufficient to defend and protect people's safety from the aggressor, authority will limit itself to such means . . . Today, in fact, as a consequence of the possibilities which the state has for effectively preventing crime [and] rendering one who has committed and offense incapable of doing harm . . . the cases in which the execution of an offender is an absolute necessity are very rare if not practically non-existent. (CCC 2267).* Hence the current resurgence in America of recourse to the death penalty is quite problematic from the standpoint of Catholic teaching. In this context we should remember the story of Cain cited above. Despite his murder of Abel, God forbade others from taking Cain's life to avenge Abel's death. Non-lethal but permanent exile, (a type of imprisonment) was the punishment God assigned.

"Just" War

Sometimes Nations face unjust aggression from other nations or groups. Legitimate Governments have the duty and right to repel aggressors by armed force if necessary (see *CCC* 2266). Here as well, recourse to military action and the use of lethal force to repel unjust aggressors must be an absolutely last recourse. Likewise, the threat posed must be of a very serious (grave) nature. If a military response is made it must be one that is carefully measured. The use of excessive force cannot be justified. Likewise, the death of non-combatants can never be directly intended. Once the threat is repelled the use of lethal force must stop. Clearly, the use of lethal force merely for retribution is entirely to be excluded. (*cf. CCC* 2307–2317).

Extended implications

The fifth commandment, while encompassing the right to self-defense of individuals and society, clearly prohibits the direct and intentional killing we call murder. The fifth commandment [also] indirectly bringing about a person's death; for example, exposing someone to grave danger without serious reason, or refusing reasonable assistance to a person in danger (see *CCC* 2269).

Acting in a reckless, violent or dangerous fashion also violates this commandment insofar as it endangers the lives of others.

Further, those who indulge greed or support and profit from injustices that lead to the hunger and death of others indirectly commit homicide for which they will be accountable to God. (*cf.* Am 8:4–10).

Abortion

Human life must be respected from the moment of conception (see *CCC* 2270). The Scriptures clearly teach that life in the womb is in God's hands and is His own handiwork: *For thou didst form my inward parts, thou didst knit me together in my mother's womb* (Ps 139:13). No human life is an accident, it is always directly intended by God and is a sovereign act of his love: *Before I formed you in the womb I knew you and before you were born I consecrated you* (Jer 1:5). For these reasons the life of the child in the womb is absolutely sacred. The child's right to life is inalienable and must never be violated. No amount of legal, political, medical, or philosophical argumentation can usurp the child's rights or God's sole sovereignty. The issue of abortion is a very painful one for our modern age. It is also an issue which tests our character. The fifth commandment obliges all members of society to uphold the gift of life by assisting and supporting pregnant women, especially those with difficult pregnancies.

Euthanasia

Euthanasia consists in directly putting an end to the lives of handicapped, sick, or dying persons. It is morally unacceptable (see *CCC* 2277). In recent years a false compassion has developed among some who hold that suffering is incompatible with human dignity. Clearly this is at odds with the Christian faith, which sees in suffering a redemptive and transformative dimension. St. Paul learned an important truth about his own suffering: *Three times I besought the Lord about this, that it should leave me; but he said to me, "My grace is sufficient for you, for my power is made perfect in weakness." I will all the more gladly boast of my weaknesses, that the power of Christ may rest upon me. For the sake of Christ, then, I am content with weaknesses, insults, hardships, persecutions, and calamities; for when I am weak, then I am strong* (2 Cor 12:8–10). It is not that Christians must relish suffering. Where possible we should seek to alleviate suffering. Yet we may never do this in ways which violate the sovereignty of God over life or which refuse the cross in an absolute sense, *Whoever does not take up his own cross and come after me, cannot be my disciple.* (Lk 14:27). True compassion then, will move us to assist others in carrying the cross. It leads to sharing in another's pain; it does not kill the person who's suffering we cannot bear. Finally, some claim that individuals have the right to end their life and claim, "I can do as I want with my own body." But this is not what Scripture teaches, *You are not your own; you were purchased and at a price! So glorify God in your body.* (1 Cor 6:20). Thus an intended act or omission of required care which causes death, even if to eliminate suffering, constitutes murder and is contrary to the dignity of the human person and to sovereignty of God over human life. (see *CCC* 2277)

Trust God

Human life is sacred. God is the author and originator of every human life and it is He who sustains every one of us. Whatever challenges it brings, life is always God's yes, and the fruit of his love. We should marvel at the awesome and mysterious gift of our own life and the life of every one we encounter. The fifth commandment then is a celebration of the gift of life. We are called not only to respect the marvelous gift of life but also to grow in trust of God and to rest in the assurance that our lives are in His hands. As usual, a song says it best: *You don't have to worry; and don't you be afraid. Joy comes in the morning; troubles they don't last always. For there's a friend named Jesus; who will wipe your tears away. So if your heart is broken; just lift your hands and pray: Oh I know that I can make it; I know that I can stand. No matter what may come my way; my life is in your hands.*

THE SIXTH COMMANDMENT

YOU SHALL NOT COMMIT ADULTERY.

Human sexuality is one of God's first and greatest gifts to the human person. It is also sacred because God himself created it and linked it with his greatest gift, the gift of life. We see its origins in the very act of our creation by God and we learn of its purpose and its glory. *So God created man in his own image, in the image of God he created him; male and female he created them. And God blessed them, and God said to them, "Be fruitful and multiply, and fill the earth and subdue it* (Gn 1:27–28). Note what this brief passage teaches us.

In the first place, man and woman are both created in God's image. Thus each of the two sexes is an image of the power and tenderness of God, possessed of equal dignity though in a different way. (see *CCC* 2335) Thus, men and women are clearly different but these sexual differences are willed by God as unique ways of reflecting his glory. These differences, far from being in opposition, compliment one another and become a source of blessing for both man and woman.

Secondly, if it is true that man and woman individually reflect God's glory it is even more the case that, united together in marriage, they are an image of God, showing forth in human flesh the Creator's generosity and fruitfulness. (see *CCC* 2335). In the Genesis account above God immediately links the distinction of the sexes to the generation of new human life: *Be fruitful and multiply*. (Gn 1:28). God is a community of persons and his love bears fruit in creation and new life. So also a man and a woman united in marriage as a community of persons literally see their love bear fruit in the generation of new life.

Sexuality is Sacred

The human person is therefore sacred and sexuality is an essential part of our holiness for through it we image God who is love and whose love is both communal and fruitful. Human sexuality is also sacred because it is from the sexual union of man and woman that every human person by God's grace is conceived and born.

The Sixth Commandment is a solemn affirmation of the dignity and holiness of human sexuality. Marital love and sexuality are upheld and honored especially by the wording of this commandment. However, the sixth commandment is not merely a commandment that prohibits the breaking of marriage vows. Otherwise it would apply only to the married. Jesus makes this point quite clear in the Sermon on the Mount: *You have heard that it was said, 'You shall not commit adultery.' But I say to you that every one who looks at a woman lustfully has already committed adultery with her in her heart.* (Mt 5:27–28) Jesus teaches that the sixth commandment concerns purity of heart and binds "every one." It prohibits lust in all its forms. And although Jesus gives the example of a man looking lustfully at a woman, he surely intends the teaching for women as well. So, the sixth commandment encompasses the whole of human sexuality. (see *CCC* 2336). So everyone is commanded by God to live chastely. That is to say, each one of us is called to sexual purity, not only of the body but also of the mind and heart. For those who are married, this means that they are called to live in absolute fidelity to one another.

For those who are unmarried sexual purity means that they must abstain from all genital sexual contact without exception. There are more specific implications regarding the sixth commandment which will be explained. But first we must understand what is meant by lust.

What is Lust?

The teaching of Jesus can seem quite severe. Most all of us have the experience of noticing that others are attractive. A man, for example, may experience an attraction to a beautiful woman even though she is not his spouse. Is this a sin? No, not in itself. In fact it is a healthy, even holy response to rejoice in the beauty of which God himself is the author. Where the sin of lust begins to enter the picture is if the man begins intentionally to fantasize sexually about a woman who is not his spouse. This involves more than non-voluntary or passing sexual thoughts that are quickly dismissed. Lust involves sexual fantasies that are willfully entertained. Lust reduces sexuality to a pleasure in itself, apart from the relationship of communion with the whole person. Sexuality is not something simply biological. It involves the innermost being of the human person. It is realized in a truly human way only in the context of marital love wherein a man and woman commit themselves totally to one another until death (see *CCC* 2361). Lust reduces persons to sexual objects and does not respect their totality. The teaching of the Sixth Commandment and our Lord Jesus is that the whole person must be loved and respected. Before sexual relations take place every one must be able to say, "I will not seek to enter into this deepest of personal communions with you without first giving you the gift of my entire life until death do us part. You are worth this much and more." Anything less cheapens sexuality and the human person.

Particular Sins against the 6th Commandment

All sins against the sixth commandment fail in some respect to reverence human person and human sexuality. **Masturbation** is the deliberate stimulation of the genital organs in order to derive sexual pleasure. By its very nature it involves the sexual fantasizing forbidden by our Lord (*cf.* Mt 5:28). It also, because it involves fantasy, tends to lead to unrealistic or selfish notions of sexuality. Further, masturbation can seriously damage the self-control so necessary in regard to sexuality by indulging the notion that sexual desires must always be satisfied. For all these same reasons, the use of **pornography** must be entirely excluded.

Fornication is carnal union between an unmarried man and an unmarried woman. Such activity is frequently and strongly condemned in the scriptures: *Be sure of this, that no fornicator or impure person, or one who is covetous (that is, an idolater), has any inheritance in the kingdom of Christ and of God. Let no one deceive you with empty words, for it is because of these things that the wrath of God comes upon the sons of disobedience.* (Eph 5:5–7). (see also: Gal 5:16–21; Rev 21:5–8; Rev 22:14–16; Mt 15:19–20; 1 Cor 6:9–20; Col 3: 5–6; 1 Thess 4:1–8; 1 Tim 1:8–11; Heb 13:4). Those who struggle with such sins should not despair of God's loving mercy. Surely God's wrath is a strong medicine intended primarily for the unrepentant that they may return to their senses. It is in fact a tragic feature of the modern age that many have simply declared fornication to be acceptable behavior. Such a position is unbiblical. The plain biblical teaching is that fornication is a sin and if it is committed it must be confessed and repented of. Enormous pain results from the rejection of

God's law. Consider the sorrows resulting from fornication: venereal diseases, AIDS, teenage pregnancy, abortion, unwed mothers left to raise their children alone, absent and/or irresponsible fathers, children unjustly deprived of a complete family. It is reported that the leading cause of poverty in this nation is single motherhood. And then there difficult to measure pain caused by broken hearts: those who have been used as sexual objects then discarded, those who have been betrayed, those who have paid a heavy price for their own transgressions. Finally, as fornication has spread, marriage itself has suffered a heavy toll. Divorce rates have skyrocketed in the modern age. There are numerous factors at work in this but it is clear that the climate of sexual promiscuity has strongly contributed to the breakdown of marriage and the family. All of these reflections help us to understand that God's forbiddance of fornication makes sense and we are reminded again that his Law was not given to take away our fun but to protect us from the evil one.

Rape which is the forcible violation of the sexual intimacy of an individual is gravely wrong. It violates the respect, freedom, and physical and moral integrity to which every person has a right. Graver still is the sexual abuse of children by adults whom the children should be able to trust and respect. Not only does this harm and violate the physical and moral integrity of the children, it also does serious psychological and emotional damage.

Prostitution also involves a serious degradation of the human person and of the gift of sexuality for those who engage in it and those who pay for it. Likewise the pornographic industry from printed materials to live shows and films is gravely sinful and does serious harm to the dignity of the human person and human sexuality. To receive or purchase any of these "services" is never permitted for a Christian. While it is always gravely sinful to engage in any of these practices the blameworthiness of the offense can be lessened if the person is forced to this humiliation by destitution.

For the married, any instance of **adultery** is obviously prohibited by the sixth commandment. This involves the mind and heart as well as the body.

Another teaching of the Church which is certain even if it is unpopular with some is that artificial **contraception** is not permitted. Recall that when God gave the gift of human sexuality. He linked it directly to the mandate to be fruitful and multiply (*cf.* Gn 1:27–28). For this reason the Church teaches that it is wrong to engage in the marriage act while intentionally excluding an openness to the possibility of new human life.

Homosexuality *refers to relations between men or between women who experience an exclusive or predominant sexual attraction toward persons of the same sex . . . Basing itself on Sacred Scripture, which presents homosexual acts as acts of grave depravity,*(cf Gn 19:1–29; Rom 1:24–27; 1 Cor 6:10; 1 Tim 1:10) [the Church] *has always declared that homosexual acts are intrinsically disordered.* (CCC 2357). It must be said however that most men and women of homosexual orientation did not choose their homosexual orientation. *For most of them it is a trial. They must be accepted with respect, compassion, and sensitivity. Every sign of unjust discrimination in their regard should be avoided* (CCC 2358). Scriptures do not permit a different law of chastity for those of homosexual orientation. Like every human person, they are called to chastity and since they are unmarried they must live celibately just as is the case for heterosexual singles. This may seem challenging but it is also a teaching of our faith that God never requires of anyone what he does not first give the grace to accept and live.

God's grace is perhaps the best point on which to conclude all these teachings. There is little doubt that many of these teachings on sexuality are challenging. But the Church presents them to us in the confidence of God's grace. God has called us to freedom and the truth about our passions is that either we will rule our passions or they shall rule us. God offers us the graces necessary to overcome all temptation and to develop self-mastery. Self-mastery is a long and exacting work. On the way to receiving this gift fully from God there will often be setbacks and falls. Yet God is rich in mercy and continues to call us home. If we make this journey with humility and repentance we need never doubt his patience and mercy. The Sixth Commandment is God's yes to our freedom and to the dignity and beauty of his gift to us, the gift of our sexuality.

THE SEVENTH COMMANDMENT

YOU SHALL NOT STEAL.

At first glance this commandment seems pretty simple and straight-forward: "Don't take anything that doesn't belong to you without permission." True enough, the seventh commandment does call us to respect the rights of others in regard to their personal property. This understanding however, is incomplete. The seventh commandment has very far-reaching implications by calling upon everyone to act with justice in regards to the goods of this world. For example, take note of the following quote from the *Catechism of the Catholic Church* and see how wide ranging the sins against the seventh Commandment are: *The seventh commandment forbids theft, that is,* [unjustly taking or keeping] another's *property against the reasonable will of the owner . . . deliberate retention of goods lent or of objects lost; business fraud; paying unjust wages; forcing up prices by taking advantage of the ignorance or hardship of another . . . appropriation and use for private purposes of the common goods of an enterprise; work poorly done; tax evasion; forgery of checks and invoices; excessive expenses and waste. Willfully damaging private or public property is also contrary to the moral law and requires reparation.* (CCC 2408–2409)

Thus, while the seventh commandment clearly involves questions of the rights to personal property, it has extensive social justice implications as well since the unjust distribution of goods amounts to a form of theft. In order to understand the social justice implications of this commandment it is necessary to consider some principles regarding creation and our stewardship of it.

The universal destination of goods

The first principle is what the catechism calls the "universal destination of goods." This means that in setting forth the goods of creation God intends them for the whole human race. And thus, I should regard the things I legitimately own not merely as our mine to be used exclusively by me, but common to others also, in such a way that these things can benefit them. We are not really owners; we are stewards of what belongs to God. We have the task of making what we receive from God fruitful and beneficial to others, first of to our family and extending outward as well. (see *CCC* 2402, 2404).

A steward is expected manage the properties under his care according to the true owner's instructions and manifest wishes. In countless passages of the Old Testament as well as the New, God commands us to a generous stewardship of his creation. We are not to hoard things or be selfish. We are to share the goods we have received with others. This is particularly true for those who have strong influence in the economy or who have received special business-related skills. Thus those who have received stewardship over the goods of production such as land, factories, Internet domains, etc., or have practical or artistic skills, are obliged to use and deploy them in ways that benefit the greatest number. (see *CCC* 2405)

The Catechism, while acknowledging the right to private property justly acquired, nevertheless emphasizes that such property rights must be understood in the light of the universality of God's gifts to the whole of mankind: The concept and right to private property, does not overrule the original gift of the earth to the whole of mankind. (see *CCC* 2403).

The principle of moderation

A second principle in the possession and use of goods is moderation. Greed is the insatiable desire for more and it leads some to hoard the goods of this earth or to squander them for selfish purposes. We should reserve generous portions of what we have for guests, for the sick and the poor. (see *CCC* 2405). Greed not only leads to an unjust distribution of goods, it also frequently leads to harmful effects through pollution and to the dissipation of resources. In addition, moderation is not only a virtue for the present time, it also regards the future. And therefore *The seventh commandment also summons us to respect for creation. Natural resources, are by nature destined for the common good of past, present, and future humanity. [cf Gn 1:28–31] Our dominion over creation is not absolute. It must be governed by concern for the quality of life of others, including generations to come.* (see *CCC* 2415)

Injustice is a form of theft

It is evident that to willfully neglect either the principle of moderation or the principle of the "universal destination of goods" amounts to a form of theft. This is because it neglects the just distribution of goods, which God gave for all.

Thus, the seventh commandment is about more than protecting personal property rights. It also upholds the need for justice and charity in the care and use of earthly goods. Care and concern for the poor should be considered an integral part of the justice and charity to which we are called.

The seventh commandment and the social doctrine of the Church

The seventh commandant also provides an important basis for the social doctrine of the Church. This is an important body of Church moral teaching regarding economic and social matters and how they relate to the fundamental rights of the human person. There is simply not enough room in this context to consider all these moral teachings in detail. The heart of these teachings however is always to emphasize the rights and the dignity of the human person. This dignity must never be undermined by considerations that are purely economic or where profit is the only norm and end of economic activity. In all her pronouncements the Church has steered a middle course that has found much to critique in communism and capitalism as well as other ideologies and economic theories. Regulating the economy solely by centralized planning perverts the basis of social bonds and violates subsidiarity. However regulating it solely by the law of the marketplace fails justice, for there are many human needs, which cannot be satisfied by the market. Thus the Church commends reasonable regulation of the marketplace and economic initiatives, if such regulation is in keeping with a just hierarchy of values and the common good. (see *CCC* 2425).

There are other matters relating to the social doctrine of the church that flow from the seventh commandment. To intentionally neglect them amounts also to a form of theft: failing to pay a just wage, failing to perform a just day's work for a just day's wage, engaging in unfair or unjustly discriminatory hiring practices, and any form of subordinating basic human rights to production schedules or market forces.

The duty to work

Every Christian has the duty of work. This duty proceeds from the fact that we are created in the image of God and called to continue the work of creation by "subduing the earth," (*cf.* Gn 1:28) So work is a duty. Scripture says: "If any one will not work, let him not eat." (2 Thes 3:10) Work honors the fact that God has given us talents and abilities. Work is also redemptive for us. (see *CCC* 2427)

Clearly "work" here refers to more than a wage-paying job. Work includes all the ways in which we are expected to contribute to household and community tasks. It must be recalled that God expects us to put our gifts, which we have received from him at the service of one another. The refusal to work is a form of theft since it robs the human community of necessary human resources, deprives it of gifts God has given, and all the while still draws on the fruits of others' labors. This reflection clearly presupposes that one is able to work in some fashion and not prevented from contributing to the human family due to illness of some other serious reason.

Respect for the goods of others

Our work is not only a blessing for the community; it is also a blessing for the individual and his or her family. For this reason, the seventh commandment also protects and honors the fruits of our labor. Human beings should be able to benefit from the work they do in order to provide for themselves and their family. And while the goods of creation are given to the whole human race, the earth is necessarily divided up among people. So, the acquiring of property is legitimate since it helps motivate work, it reflects the dignity of persons, and helps them to meet their basic needs and the needs of those in his charge. (see *CCC* 2402, 2428). Hence the personal or "private" property of individuals that is justly attained is to be respected by others. It is not to be used by others without the explicit permission of the one to whom it belongs. If it is damaged intentionally or by accident, reparation must be made. By respecting the property of others we honor their freedom and dignity. We also acknowledge respect the duties of others when we respect their property for it is out of the fruits of their labors that they must support their family and meet their obligations to the community. In this way respect for private property is also related to the common good.

The call to respect our neighbors' goods is ultimately a call to respect our neighbor. In this way the seventh commandment, like all the others, is a solemn reaffirmation of the dignity of the human person. By setting forth our responsibilities with regard to this world's goods God calls us to honor our neighbor, he also reminds us of the nobility of our call to be stewards of his creation.

THE EIGHTH COMMANDMENT

YOU SHALL NOT BEAR FALSE WITNESS
AGAINST YOUR NEIGHBOR.

The Eighth Commandment proclaims the splendor and the beauty of the truth. It is not often that we hear of the truth described in this way but consider how precious and essential a foundation the truth is for our lives. Without the truth there can be no trust and without trust there can be no relationships with others. Without the truth there is cynicism, fear, and an atmosphere of exclusion and secrecy. Without the truth lives are ruined or lost by error and falsehood. Without the truth countless men, women, and children are misled by deceitful and destructive philosophies that sow confusion and error. Jesus declared just how important and essential the truth is by describing it as the fundamental purpose of his saving mission: *For this I was born, and for this I have come into the world, to bear witness to the truth.* (Jn 18:37). Jesus also taught, *If you continue in my word, you are truly my disciples, and you will know the truth, and the truth will make you free.* (Jn 8:31)

Dedication to the truth

The first implication of the eighth commandment flows from the importance and essential nature of the truth: Christians must be dedicated to the truth and live according to it. The Old Testament attests that God is the source of all truth. His Word is truth. His Law is truth. His "faithfulness endures to all generations." (Ps 119:90; Prv 8:7; 2 Sm 7:28; Ps 119:142) Since God is "true," the members of his people are called to reflect this and live in the truth. To his disciples Jesus teaches the unconditional love of truth: "Let what you say be simply 'Yes or No.'" (Mt 5:37) (*CCC* 2465–2466).

Witness to the truth

Not only are to be dedicated to the truth and to love it, we are to witness to it by word and deed. This is particularly the case with the truth of our faith, the truth that has set us free. So we are to witness to the faith in words and deeds. Witnesses establish the truth or make it known based on what they have seen and heard. By the example of our lives we attest to the new life we received in Baptism and to reveal the power of the power of God to change and perfect us. (see *CCC* 2472) Scripture bids us, *Put off your old nature which belongs to your former manner of life and is corrupt through deceitful lusts, and be renewed in the spirit of your minds, and put on the new nature, created after the likeness of God in true righteousness and holiness. Therefore, putting away falsehood, let every one speak the truth with his neighbor, for we are members one of another.* (Eph 4:22–25) Since the eighth commandment upholds the goodness and beauty of the truth we must avoid all sins against the truth. There are numerous ways that the truth is undermined. It will be fruitful for us to consider them each in turn.

False Witness

Scripture says, *A man who bears false witness against his neighbor is like a war club, or a sword, or a sharp arrow.* (Prv 25:18) Nothing can be so injurious to individuals as to harm their good name or reputation. Without a good reputation it becomes difficult for an individual to successfully relate to and interact with others whether it be for business or merely at a personal level. Clearly, to bear false witness against someone is to harm his or her reputation and we are forbidden to do so. In the technical sense, false witness is something, which takes place in a court of law, and since it is under oath it is also called perjury. But it is also often the case that false witness is given in daily matters through lies, half-truths, exaggeration, and the like. Clearly our call to love the truth and to respect the reputation of others forbids us engaging in such activities.

Respect for the reputation of others also forbids us from: *rash judgment* (assuming without sufficient foundation the moral fault of a neighbor), *detraction* (disclosing another's faults and failings without a valid reason to others who did not know them) and *calumny* (imputing false defects to another with the knowledge that they are false).

Yet it is also possible to offend the truth by inappropriately praising others or by refusing to correct them when it is proper to do so. Flattery distorts the truth when it falsely attributes certain good qualities or talents to another. This is usually done to ingratiate oneself to individuals or for some other ulterior motive(s). Such behavior becomes particularly sinful when it confirms another in malicious acts or sinful conduct.

Lying

A lie consists in speaking something we know is false with the intention of deceiving. This is the most direct offense against the truth. Others have the right to know the truth. In lying we harm another person's relation to truth and to others. It affects his or her ability to know, which is the foundation of every judgment and decision. The Lord denounces lying as the work of the devil: *"You are of your father the devil, . . . there is no truth in him. When he lies, he speaks according to his own nature, for he is a liar and the father of lies."* (Jn 8:44) Lying offends the very purpose of speech, which is to communicate truth to others. Lying is destructive of community since it harms trust and thus tears at the fabric of social relationships. (see *CCC* 2482–2485)

Acts of lying are sins from which we must repent. Lying is also a sin that demands reparation. That is to say, since lying causes actual harm and real damage. These damages must be repaired. The actual truth must be made known to those who deserve to know it. The reputations of others, which have been harmed by the lie, must also be restored.

Is lying always so evil?

The seriousness of a lie is gauged by the nature of the truth it harms and also by the circumstances in which it occurs, the intentions of the one who lies, and the harm suffered by victims of the lie. (see *CCC* 2484). Thus there are big lies and smaller ones. Nevertheless, it is always wrong to intentionally lie. This includes so-called "polite lies." For example suppose a phone call comes in for someone in the household who has indicated a preference not to be disturbed just now. It is a lie to say, "She is not here." Yet you could say, "She is not available now." Other social situations are less simple! For example, if Mrs. Smith asks you, "Do you like my new hairstyle?" Suppose you do not. It is in fact wrong to say, "Yes, I like it." Granted, we all feel a bit stuck in such situations! Perhaps we could answer truthfully but discreetly and say, "You look alright." (Presuming that we do think so). But wouldn't it be nice if we actually felt secure enough either to indicate charitably our true feelings or to indicate our preference not to answer the question? Wouldn't it be even nicer if our relationships with others were so based in sincerity and truth that people both gave and expected honest answers? It is to this blessed state that the Lord points when he says, *Let what you say be simply 'Yes' or 'No'* (Mt 5:37).

What about secrets?

This reflection has thus far emphasized the goodness and the splendor of the truth as well as the importance of communicating that truth to others who need it. However, the right to know all things is not absolute or unconditional. The dignity of persons, and the nature of love requires some judgments and discretion about whether or not it is appropriate to reveal the truth to others merely because they want to know. There are important factors that limit us in disclosing all we know such as the good and safety of others, respect for privacy, the duty to avoid giving scandal, concern for the common good. These can supply sufficient reasons for remaining silent about what ought not be shared. It may also permit us to use discreet language. *Thus, No one is required to reveal the truth to someone who does not have the right to know it. Further all of us should observe an appropriate reserve concerning persons' private lives and reject unjust curiosity and the tendency to pass on information about others that is not necessary. This applies to those in communications media as well.*

The "people's right to know" does not necessarily extend to all the details of the private lives of even of public persons (see CCC 2488, 2489, 2492)

However, the fact that we are permitted, even obliged, to keep certain secrets and maintain discretion, does not mean that we are free to lie. For example we cannot say, "I don't know anything about that." Neither can we make up false answers to requested information. When we must decline to give information that is properly to be kept secret we must still remain truthful. We might say instead, "I am not free to discuss this matter with you now." Or, "It would be inappropriate for me to comment on that." Or, "Why don't you ask him yourself?" Occasionally we may need to be more direct and say, "This is a private matter and not for you to know."

Thus secrecy and discretion are often proper. Here too however, absolutes must be avoided. Sometimes we are asked to keep secrets that we should not keep. For example, suppose someone confides in you that they intend to commit a serious crime, or bring harm to another? It would be wrong to keep such a secret. Other things being equal secrets ought to be kept, except in cases where keeping the secret is bound to cause very grave harm, either to the one who uttered it, to the one who heard it or to some third party. If divulging the secret is the only way to avoid this harm it can be disclosed. (see *CCC* 2491).

An exception to this is the seal of confession which may never be violated for any reason whatsoever: *The sacramental seal is inviolable; therefore, it is a crime for a confessor in any way to betray a penitent by word or in any other manner or for any reason.* (*CCC* 2490).

Jesus has taught us that the truth will set us free (Jn 8:32). If this be the case then anything which distorts the truth leads to bondage. Thus the eighth commandment calls upon us to love the truth and to love one another by proclaiming the truth and witnessing to it in sincerity with mutual respect and love.

THE NINTH AND TENTH COMMANDMENTS

YOU SHALL NOT COVET YOUR
NEIGHBOR'S WIFE OR HIS GOODS.

There exists within each of us a whole range of appetites or desires. We desire everything from food, security, and temporal goods, to affection, friendship, sexual union, and a sense of being loved and respected. In themselves these desires are good and they help protect and foster important aspects of ourselves. However, since the human race labors under the effects of original sin, our desires tend also to have an unruly dimension. Frequently we desire things beyond what we know is reasonable or just. This is what is meant by coveting. Coveting does not include momentary desires that occur to us and which we dismiss as being unreasonable or inappropriate. Rather, coveting involves the willful entertaining of inappropriate or excessive desires.

The importance of self control

A significant truth about our desires and passions is that if we overindulge them they become more and more demanding and powerful in their influences over our conduct. Self-control becomes increasingly difficult to those who are self-indulgent. If we do not learn to temper our desires they quickly dominate us. Our dignity therefore summons us to act out of conscious and free choice. We are not to be brute animals governed by blind impulses. Our dignity is to be free from all slavery to the passions and excessive desires. (see *CCC* 2339). The ninth and tenth commandments remind us of our freedom and dignity and solemnly instruct us in the importance of self control in terms of our desires. The significance of this issue for our well-being and happiness is emphasized by the fact that two commandments are devoted to matters of covetousness. We shall look at them each in turn.

The ninth commandment:
You shall not covet your neighbor's wife.

Much has already been said of the importance of sexual purity when we considered the sixth commandment. It is not necessary to repeat all that material here. In terms of the ninth commandment the essential call is for the individual by the grace of God to attain purity of heart. The heart is innermost place of the human person and the place we deliberate. The battle against covetousness centers on purifying the heart and practicing temperance (see *CCC* 2517). To be pure in heart, means that we have attuned our mind and heart to the demands of holiness. It means we have purified our desires so that we keep God's law not because we have to, but because we want to.

This may seem difficult since our desires do not usually change in an instant. Just because we know that our heart desires things or persons in ways that are excessive or inappropriate does not make these desires disappear. Yet through consistent self-discipline, custody of the eyes and the other senses, recourse to prayer and sacraments, all with the help of God's grace, the desires of our heart change. We begin to love what God loves. What is sinful becomes less tempting and the thought of sin eventually becomes even abhorrent to us. By God's grace our hearts change so that we can sing, *Well I'm not what I want to be but I'm not what I used to be, What a wonderful change has come over me.*

The purification of our desires.

Clearly this change in our desires involves an increasing self-discipline. In terms of sexuality we must guard our eyes and ears from suggestive or obscene things. We must exercise discipline over our feelings and our imagination by refusing to consent to the impure thoughts and desires that tempt us. In addition we will avoid situations with particular individuals which we know are tempting and we will dress and conduct ourselves modestly. As we exercise such self-discipline we discover our freedom and grow in that freedom through God's grace. We will also discover that what we truly desire comes more and more into line with God's commandants and his will for us.

Consequences

Refusing to do these things and yielding to covetous sexual desires leads to unhappy, even tragic consequences. Consider the example of King

David who coveted Bathsheba, the wife of Uriah the Hittite. He yielded to his covetous desires, slept with her and she became pregnant as a result. David, embarrassed at his predicament, contrived to have Uriah killed in order to have Bathsheba as his own and to hide his adulterous conduct. Yielding to covetous sexual desires does not always lead to such dramatic results but it never leads to good results or produces lasting happiness. Our own age has witnessed a considerable rebellion against the ninth commandment and we have had to reap the sad consequences we discussed when we considered the sixth commandment. The ninth commandment seeks to protect us from the dangers of unrestrained sexual desire. It also invites us to discover the freedom that God's grace will bring fully alive and the joy that purity of heart can bring.

The Tenth Commandment:
You shall not covet your neighbors goods.

Since it is the last of the Ten Commandments, it is fitting that the tenth commandment flow from and complete many of the other commandments. It forbids coveting the goods of another, which is at the root of theft, robbery, and fraud, which the seventh commandment forbids. Coveting, or "lust of the eyes" as scripture calls it (1 Jn 2:16) many times leads to the violence and injustice forbidden by the fifth commandment. Likewise, greed, which is very closely tied to covetousness, originates in the idolatry prohibited by the first three commandments. This is because of the way that covetousness frequently leads to a kind of worship of material goods.

The tenth commandment also completes the ninth since coveting involves far more than sexual matters. The scriptures specify the wide scope of coveting: *You shall not covet your neighbor's house; you shall not covet. your neighbor's wife, or his man-servant, or his maidservant, or his ox, or his ass, or anything that is your neighbor's."* (Ex 20:17). The ninth commandment forbids coveting in regard to sexual desires. The tenth commandment forbids all other forms of coveting.

We should recall that coveting by definition involves the willful entertaining of excessive or inappropriate desires. Thus, it is not wrong to desire the things we reasonably need. Clearly it is essential for our survival that we desire food, water, warmth, and shelter. Love, affection, family, and work are also essential for us and it is proper that we desire and seek fulfillment in these areas. Even seemingly non-essential things like recreation and entertainment are in fact necessary ingredients in life and our desire for such things is an important aspect of every healthy person. So long as our desires for any of these things is not unreasonable and we do not seek to fulfill them in inappropriate ways we can say that they are good, even holy aspects of the human person.

Greed.

The tenth commandment forbids greed, which is the desire to amass earthly goods without limit. It also forbids avarice which is an undue passion for riches and power. (see *CCC* 2536).

Envy and jealousy.

The tenth commandment also requires that envy be banished. Envy is refers to the sadness at the sight of another's goods or excellence because I take it to lessen my own standing before others. It is different than jealousy (which is the immoderate desire to posses (even unjustly) the goods or excellences of another). When I am jealous of you, you have something I want. But when I am envious of you, you have something good I want to destroy. For this reason, St. Augustine saw envy as <u>the</u> diabolical sin: "From envy are born hatred, detraction, calumny, joy caused by the misfortune of a neighbor, and displeasure caused by his prosperity." (see *CCC* 2538–2539). In this context it is worth noting scripture's teaching, Through the devil's envy, death entered the world. (Ws 2:24).

The tenth commandment, like all the commandments calls us higher. It calls us to recognize the freedom and the healing which God offers us through his grace. For in terms of our passions and desires we can easily become enslaved. How easily we become inebriated with the things of this world and become trapped by the seemingly insatiable desire for more. One look at the credit card balances of many Americans reveals that we live beyond our means and have difficulty controlling our desires. In some cases individuals are unable or unwilling to delay gratifications. Others consider as essential, things which they could do without. The tenth commandment calls us away from the illusions of necessity and immediacy. We are summoned to a freedom which recognizes that we can discipline our desires and master our passions so that we make sound, wise, and just decisions in acquiring and using the goods of this world.

What are our desires really saying?

As we master our passions and desires we also learn more clearly what they are truly saying to us. Fundamentally every desire represents a deeper longing for God who is the giver of every good gift. In the deepest part of our heart there is a song, *I'd rather have Jesus, then silver or gold.* The tragedy is that many become lost searching for happiness in the things of this world. This ends in frustration and emptiness for our deepest longings are infinite. The finite things of the world cannot fulfill the infinite longings of our heart. For this reason Jesus teaches us to prefer him to everything and everyone, and calls us to renounce all we have for his sake and that of the Gospel. (Lk 14:33). Detachment from riches is obligatory for entrance into the Kingdom of Heaven ... Jesus laments rich, because they find their consolation in the abundance of goods. (Lk 6:24) which cannot ultimately save them. But blessed are the poor in spirit for theirs is the Kingdom of heaven." (Mt 5:2) (See *CCC* 2544, 2547).

In the end, the tenth commandment calls us away from idolatry of worldly things and to the worship of the one, true God just as did the first commandment. It also calls us to abandonment to the providence of God and to freedom from anxiety about tomorrow which fuels so much of our desires to hoard and control the things of this world. Finally, it summons us to a desire for the true happiness which frees us from attachment to the goods of this world. For, once we have authentically tasted the Lord and experienced how good he is, our desires for many other things quietly abate and covetousness melts away. *I heard my mother say, 'Give me Jesus. You may have all this world. Just give me Jesus.'*

An Examination of Conscience Rooted in the Ten Commandments:

FIRST COMMANDMENT

"I am the Lord your God. You shall not have strange gods before Me." (Ex 20:2,3)

- Did I doubt or deny that God exists?

- Did I refuse to believe what God has revealed to us?

- Did I believe in fortune telling, horoscopes, dreams, the occult, good-luck charms, tarot cards, palmistry, Ouija boards, seances, reincarnation?

- Did I deny that I was Catholic?

- Did I leave the Catholic Faith?

- Did I give time to God each day in prayer?

- Did I love God with my whole heart?

- Did I despair of or presume on God's mercy?

- Did I have false gods in my life that I gave greater attention to than God, like money, profession, drugs, TV, fame, pleasure, property, etc.?

- Do I exhibit the obedience of faith my striving to wholeheartedly apply God's truths to my life

- Do I sincerely Drive to grow in my knowledge of the faith which God has revealed?

- Do I exhibit proper priorities in my life that exhibit God's sovereignty in my life

- Do I pray each day and seek to carefully listen to the Lords direction?

- Is my love and worship of God sincere and deeply interior, or is it merely external and perfunctory observance.

- Do I trust God, or do I seek in
  many ways to manipulate the future,
  by controlling attitudes, The lack
  of submission, or superstitious
  practices.

- As a believer, have I contributed
  to the rise of atheism but the poor
  example I give of living the faith?

- Do I abuse the freedom God is
  giving me, or have an exaggerated
  sense of my autonomy.

- Do I struggle with the sin of human
  respect, wherein I care more for
  what human beings think of me and
  what God thinks?

- And my willing to suffer for my
  faith in small and daily ways, as well
  as, if necessary with my life?

- Do I make reasonable attempts to
  refute errors regarding God was
  a face that heater expressed in
  my family, or among friends and
  acquaintances?

- Do I contribute, through evangelization efforts to draw others to faith in
  the one true God?

SECOND COMMANDMENT

"You shall not take the Name of the Lord your
God in vain." (Ex 20:7)

- Have I used God's name or the name
  of the Lord Jesus to curse, condemn,
  or the berate others?

- Have I blasphemed God by uttering
  words of hatred, reproach or defiance against him?

- Do I too easily expose myself to
  movies, books, and other sources
  where the Divine Name is abused,
  or other foul language is prevalent?

- Do I use God's name in vain, that is
  empty ways, with expressions such
  as "Oh my God!" or, "Lord!" or, "I
  swear to God!" ?

- Have I sworn false oaths?

- Do I keep my promises, vows, and oaths?

- Do I make promises and oaths too easily or lightly?

- Do I speak God's name with praise?

- Am I grateful to God for revealing his name so as to build intimacy and trust with me?

THIRD COMMANDMENT

"Remember that you keep holy the Sabbath Day." (Ex 20:8)

- Do I see my obligation to rest on Sunday as rooted in my dignity as one made in the image of God who rested?

- Do I do work on Sunday that is not necessary?

- Do I strive to set aside Sunday as a day of rest and a family day?

- Do I do unnecessary shopping or other activities that distract from my need to rest or that of others to rest?

- Did I miss Mass Sunday or a Holy Day of Obligation without a serious reason and through my own fault?

- Do I get to Mass on time? Do I leave early?

- Do I participate in the Sacred Liturgy with devotion and attentiveness?

- Do I show reverence in the Lord's presence?

- Do I dress modestly, and appropriately for Mass?

- If I am a parent or elder, do impress on younger people in my care the need to get to Mass? Do I insist they go?

- Am I grateful to God and mindful of all he has done for me? Or do I merely go to Church out of obligation or because I am pressured to go?

- Do I prepare in any way for Mass, or just rush there at the last minute?

- Do I receive the Sacrament of Holy Communion in a state of grace?

- Do I make proper praise and thanksgiving after receiving Communion.

- Do I ever reflect on the blessings of the Sacred Liturgy in my life?

- Do I ever discuss with others, my children, family, or friends, the blessings received at Mass?

- Did I fast on Ash Wednesday and Good Friday?

- Did I eat meat on the Fridays of Lent or Ash Wednesday?

- Did I fail to receive Holy Communion during Eastertime?

FOURTH COMMANDMENT

"Honor your father and your mother." (Ex 20:12)

- Did I disobey or disrespect my parents, elders, or legitimate superiors?

- Did I neglect my duties to my husband, wife, children, or parents?

- Did I neglect to give good religious example to my family?

- Did I fail to actively take an interest in the religious education and formation of my children?

- Am I open to being taught by others, especially elders?

- Did I give scandal by what I said or did, especially to the young?

- Do I seek to protect my children and family from degrading and sinful influences?

- Do I encourage my children and spouse? Do I show affection?

- Did I cause anyone to leave the faith?

- Did I cause tension and fights in my family? Do I actively promote harmony?

- Have I failed to forgive anyone in my family?

- Do I show gratitude to my family members, especially my elders?

- Have I properly cared for my aged and infirm relatives?

- Do I promote respect for traditional Marriage and family?

- Do I honor and pray for all in lawful authority?

- Do I have a healthy love and support for my Country?

- Do I love the Church and support my parish?

FIFTH COMMANDMENT

"You shall not kill." (Ex 20:13)

- Do I regard all human life as Sacred, as belonging to God?

- Did I kill or physically injure anyone?

- Did I endanger anyone's life or physical well being by reckless or dangerous behaviors?

- Have I acted in violent ways or pro-voked violent anger in others?

- Have I been impatient, envious, unkind, revengeful, jealous, or hateful toward others?

- Have I engaged in fighting, or quarreling?

- Do I view movies or play video games that feature gratuitous violence, make light of human life, or celebrate violent killing.

- Did I use illegal drugs, drink alcohol to excess such that I endangered myself or others?

- Do I respect my own life, health, and well-being?

- Do I help to preserve the life of the vulnerable by helping the poor and needy according to my means?

- Did I have an abortion, or assist or advise someone else to have an abortion?

- Do I pray to end abortion and euthanasia?

- Have I done enough to witness to the dignity of human life?

- Did I use, or cause my spouse to use, birth control pills which most often work by aborting the fetus if and when conceived?

- Did I attempt suicide?

- Did I take part in or approve of "mercy killing" (euthanasia)?

- Did I abuse my children?

- Do I seek reconciliation with those I have harmed or sinned against?

- Am I merciful and forgiving?

- Do I pray for my enemy?

- Do I work for harmony in my community, among races and ethnic groups?

- Do I pray for peace?

SIXTH COMMANDMENT

"You shall not commit adultery." (Ex 20:14) "You shall not covet your neighbor's wife." (Ex 20:17)

- Did I entertain impure thoughts or desires?

- Did I use impure or suggestive words? Tell impure stories? Listen to them?

- Did I engage in impure conversations in person or on the Internet?

- Did I dress immodestly, or act immodestly by impure gestures, postures, or lewd conduct?

- Did I deliberately look at impure shows, pornography on the internet, videos, plays, pictures, or movies?

- Did I read impure materials?

- Did I commit impure acts by myself (masturbation)?

- Did I commit impure acts with another—fornication (premarital sex), adultery (sex with a married person) or homosexual acts?

- Did I pressure anyone to have illicit sex or seek to seduce anyone?

- Have I made light of Human sexuality by jokes, lewd remarks, or ridicule of chastity and purity?

- Have I sought to witness to others of sound Biblical and Holy norms for sexuality?

- Do I esteem Holy Matrimony and respect the privileges of marital sexuality?

- Did I practice artificial birth control?

- Did I marry outside the Church or advise anyone to do so?

- Did I strive to avoid the occasions of impurity and temptation?

- Did I respect all members of the opposite sex, or have I thought of other people as objects?

- Did I or my spouse get sterilized?

- Did I abuse my marriage rights?

- Have I been generous enough with my spouse and sensitive to their need for intimacy and attention?

SEVENTH & TENTH COMMANDMENTS

"You shall not steal." (Ex 20:15) "You shall not covet your neighbor's goods." (Ex 20:17)

- Did I steal, cheat, help, or encourage others to steal or keep stolen goods?

- Am I respectful of the goods of others?

- Have I made restitution for stolen goods of the property of another that I may have damaged?

- Do I pay my bills in a timely manner?

- Did I fulfill my contracts.

- Do I pay just wages?

- Have I given or accepted bribes?

- Have I deprived my family of the necessities of life by my own foolish use of money?

- Do I fulfill my duty to work and contribute to the commonwealth in accord with my abilities and state of life?

- Did I waste time at work, school, or at home?

- Did I envy other people's families or possessions?

- Did I make material possessions the purpose of my life?

- Do I hoard things or buy accumulate many things I don't really need?

- Do I help the poor? Am I mindful of my obligations to them both in justice and in charity?

- Did I fail to contribute to the support of the Church?

- Am I a generous and cheerful giver?

- Am I satisfied with and grateful for what I have?

- Is greed, the insatiable desire for more, a strong drive in me?

- Am I jealous of the goods and gifts of others?

- Do I seek to harm or undermine the gifts, talents and things of others out of envy, thinking their blessings somehow diminish me?

- Am I mindful that I am the steward of what God has entrusted to me, not the owner? Am I grateful? Do I use what I have in accord with God's wishes or merely my own?

- Am I self-controlled? If not, in what areas of my life?

- Do I seek to purify my desires and to ask God for greater self-control and moderation? When?

- Do I exhibit custody of the eyes, or am I forever reading catalogues, etc. that excite my desires for more?

- Do I allow my desires and longings to point me to God and heaven, or do I seek to satisfy them with merely worldly things and people?

- Do I waste or even squander food, water, or other resources?

- Am I respectful of the generations that will come after me, by good stewardship of resources?

EIGHTH COMMANDMENT

"You shall not bear false witness against your neighbor." (Ex 20:16)

- Did I lie?

- Did I deliberately deceive others, or injure others by lies?

- Did I commit perjury (lying under oath)?

- Did I gossip or reveal others' faults or sins?

- Have I harmed other's reputations by half truths or facts told out of context?

- Did I fail to keep secret what should be confidential?

- Have I engaged in rash judgment, assuming too quickly to be true whatever I hear?

- Have I sought to ingratiate myself to others by flattery or other false praise?

- Have I sought to correct the errors or lies I have spread if possible?

- Have I pried into matters that were none of my business?

- Do I exhibit proper discretion in sharing things, especially in the presence of children?

- Have I kept secrets when I should not have done so. For example when I was asked to cover up threats or crimes committed against others?

- Have I shared things and opinions I should not?

- Do I seek truth and try to base my life on it?

- Do I announce the truth of the Gospel by the witness of my life and my words?

- Am I willing to speak the truth charitably to others, even a significant cost? Really?

- Am I will even to die for the truth of the Gospel? Really?

- Do I fear human beings and their views more than God?

BIBLICAL
EXAMENS

The following three passages provide a biblical framework to exam our conscience:

Col 3:12ff: Put on then, as God's chosen ones, holy and beloved, compassion, kindness, lowliness, meekness, and patience, forbearing one another and, if one has a complaint against another, forgiving each other; as the Lord has forgiven you, so you also must forgive. And above all these put on love, which binds everything together in perfect harmony. And let the peace of Christ rule in your hearts, to which indeed you were called in the one body. And be thankful. Let the word of Christ dwell in you richly, teach and admonish one another in all wisdom, and sing psalms and hymns and spiritual songs with thankfulness in your hearts to

God.[17]And whatever you do, in word or deed, do everything in the name of the Lord Jesus, giving thanks to God the Father through him.

1 Corinthians 13:4ff: Love is patient and kind; love is not jealous or boastful; it is not arrogant or rude. Love does not insist on its own way; it is not irritable or resentful; it does not rejoice at wrong, but rejoices in the right. Love bears all things, believes all things, hopes all things, endures all things.

Gal 5:16ff: But I say, walk by the Spirit, and do not gratify the desires of the flesh. For the desires of the flesh are against the Spirit, and the desires of the Spirit are against the flesh; for these are opposed to each other, to prevent you from doing what you would. But if you are led by the Spirit you are not under the law.[19] Now the works of the flesh are plain: fornication, impurity, licentiousness, idolatry, sorcery, enmity, strife, jealousy, anger, selfishness, dissension, party spirit, envy, drunkenness, carousing, and the like. I warn you, as I warned you before, that those who do such things shall not inherit the kingdom of God. But the fruit of the Spirit is love, joy, peace, patience, kindness, goodness, faithfulness, gentleness, self-control; against such there is no law. And those who belong to Christ Jesus have crucified the flesh with its passions and desires.

The following litanies seek to invite us to look a little deeper into our heart. As the litany proceeds we move from external behaviors, to interior dispositions and drives, as well as sins of omission.

LITANIES OF REPENTANCE

In reparation for sins against justice
In reparation for sins against modesty.
In reparation for sins against purity.
In reparation for sins against truth.
In reparation for all sins against the human person.
In reparation for sins against children and the young.
In reparation for sins against the innocent and trusting.
In reparation for sins against the frail and elderly.
In reparation for sins against the unborn and infants.
In reparation for sins against the weak and powerless.
In reparation for sins against immigrants and strangers.
In reparation for sins against the poor and disadvantaged.

In reparation for sins against the sanctity of marriage.

In reparation for sins against the sanctity of the family.

In reparation for sins against the sanctity of the priesthood.

In reparation for sins against the sanctity of consecrated life.

For our failure to give witness to Christ as we ought.

For our failure to submit our will to God.

For our failure to give good example to others.

For our failure to seek God above all things.

For our failure to act justly.

For our failure to show mercy.

For our failure to repent of our sins.

For our failure to obey the commandments of the gospel.

For our failure to curb our earthly desires.

For our failure to lead a holy life.

For our failure to speak the truth.

For our failure to stand up against injustice.

For our failure to live chastely.

For our failure to show compassion for the suffering.

For our failure to guide sinners to repentance.

For our failure to pray for others.

For our failure to assist those in need.

For our failure to console the grieving.

For our failure to forgive others.

For our failure to encourage those who are weak in faith.

For our failure to endure the trials of life patiently.

For our failure to visit the sick.

For our failure to love as we ought.

For our failure to practice our faith with zeal.

For our failure to work for the unity of peoples and nations.

For our failure to promote peace and reconciliation.

For our failure to seek forgiveness for our sins.

For our failure to be generous with our goods.

For sins committed out of fear.

For sins committed out of indifference.

For sins committed out of contempt.

For sins committed out of impurity.

For sins committed out of hatred.

For sins committed out of laziness.

For sins committed out of cowardice.

For sins committed out of anger.

For sins committed out of greed.

For sins committed out of jealousy.
For sins committed out of revenge.
For sins committed out of disobedience.
For sins committed out of hard-heartedness.
For sins committed out of pride.
For sins committed out of envy.
For sins committed out of stinginess.
For sins committed out of selfishness.
For sins committed out of pettiness.
For sins committed out of spite.
For sins committed out of self-indulgence.
For sins committed out of lust.
For sins committed out of careless neglect.
For sins committed out of prejudice.

Because I am obnoxious, forgive me Lord.
Because I am dishonest, forgive me Lord.
Because I am egotistical, forgive me Lord.
Because I am undisciplined, forgive me Lord.
Because I am weak, forgive me Lord.
Because I am impure, forgive me Lord.
Because I am arrogant, forgive me Lord.
Because I am self-centered, forgive me Lord.
Because I am pompous, forgive me Lord.
Because I am insincere, forgive me Lord.
Because I am unchaste, forgive me Lord.
Because I am grasping, forgive me Lord.

Because I am judgmental, forgive me Lord.
Because I am impatient, forgive me Lord.
Because I am shallow, forgive me Lord.
Because I am inconsistent, forgive me Lord.
Because I am unfaithful, forgive me Lord.
Because I am immoral, forgive me Lord.
Because I am ungrateful, forgive me Lord.
Because I am disobedient, forgive me Lord.
Because I am selfish, forgive me Lord.
Because I am lukewarm, forgive me Lord.
Because I am slothful, forgive me Lord.
Because I am unloving, forgive me Lord.
Because I am uncommitted, forgive me Lord.
Because I am sinful, forgive me Lord.
Because I am loved by You, thank you Lord!

I have been unfaithful
I have been unworthy
I have been unrighteous
And I have been unmerciful
I have been unreachable
I have been unteachable
I have been unwilling
And I have been undesirable
Sometimes I have unwise
I've been undone by what I'm unsure of
But because of You

And all that You went through
I know that I have never been unloved
I have been unbroken
I have been unmended
I have been uneasy
And I've been unapproachable
I've been unemotional
I've been unexceptional
I've been undecided
And I have been unqualified
Unaware, I have been unfair
I've been unfit for blessings from above
But even I can see
The sacrifice You made for me
To show that I have never been unloved
It's because of You
And all that You went through
I know that I have never been unloved

An Act of Contrition:

O my God, I am heartily sorry for having offended
Thee, and I detest all my sins, because I dread the
loss of heaven, and the pains of hell; but most of
all because they offend Thee, my God, Who are
all good, and deserving of all my love. I firmly
resolve, with the help of Thy grace, to confess my
sins, to do penance, and to amend my life.

About the Author

Msgr. Charles Pope has a Master of Arts Degree in Moral Theology from Mount St. Mary's University, Emmitsburg, MD. He was ordained to the priesthood on June 24, 1989, and is currently a pastor in Washington DC. He has conducted a weekly Bible Studies in the U.S. Congress and the White House. He has served on the Priest Council, as an Archdiocesan Consultor, and a member of the Priest Personnel Board and is a Dean. He was named a Monsignor in 2005. Monsignor Pope publishes a daily blog, has written in pastoral journals, and offers a weekly column in *Our Sunday Visitor*. He has taught numerous catechetical courses both in his parish work, and for the Archdiocese, conducted numerous Priest retreats and also for the faithful. Monsignor Pope immensely enjoys his work as a diocesan priest and a parish pastor.

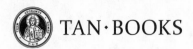

TAN·BOOKS

TAN Books was founded in 1967 to preserve the spiritual, intellectual and liturgical traditions of the Catholic Church. At a critical moment in history TAN kept alive the great classics of the Faith and drew many to the Church. In 2008 TAN was acquired by Saint Benedict Press. Today TAN continues its mission to a new generation of readers.

From its earliest days TAN has published a range of booklets that teach and defend the Faith. Through partnerships with organizations, apostolates, and mission-minded individuals, well over 10 million TAN booklets have been distributed.

More recently, TAN has expanded its publishing with the launch of Catholic calendars and daily planners—as well as Bibles, fiction, and multimedia products through its sister imprints Catholic Courses (CatholicCourses.com) and Saint Benedict Press (SaintBenedictPress.com).

Today TAN publishes over 500 titles in the areas of theology, prayer, devotions, doctrine, Church history, and the lives of the saints. TAN books are published in multiple languages and found throughout the world in schools, parishes, bookstores and homes.

For a free catalog, visit us online at
TANBooks.com

Or call us toll-free at
(800) 437-5876

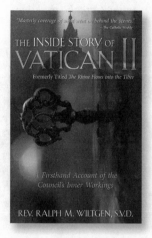

TAN·CLASSICS

*A collection of the finest literature
in the Catholic tradition.*

978-0-89555-227-3

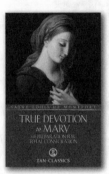

978-0-89555-154-2

978-0-89555-155-9

Our TAN Classics collection is a well-balanced sampling
of the finest literature in the Catholic tradition.

978-0-89555-230-3

978-0-89555-228-0

978-0-89555-151-1

978-0-89555-153-5

978-0-89555-149-8

978-0-89555-199-3

The collection includes distinguished spiritual works of the saints, philosophical treatises and famous biographies.

978-0-89555-226-6

978-0-89555-152-8

978-0-89555-225-9

Spread the Faith with . . .

TAN·BOOKS

A Division of Saint Benedict Press, LLC

TAN books are powerful tools for evangelization. They lift the mind to God and change lives. Millions of readers have found in TAN books and booklets an effective way to teach and defend the Faith, soften hearts, and grow in prayer and holiness of life.

Throughout history the faithful have distributed Catholic literature and sacramentals to save souls. St. Francis de Sales passed out his own pamphlets to win back those who had abandoned the Faith. Countless others have distributed the Miraculous Medal to prompt conversions and inspire deeper devotion to God. Our customers use TAN books in that same spirit.

If you have been helped by this or another TAN title, share it with others. Become a TAN Missionary and share our life changing books and booklets with your family, friends and community. We'll help by providing special discounts for books and booklets purchased in quantity for purposes of evangelization. Write or call us for additional details.

TAN Books
Attn: TAN Missionaries Department
P.O. Box 410487
Charlotte, NC 28241

Toll-free (800) 437-5876
missionaries@TANBooks.com